EMMANUEL JOSEPH

Lead with Your Voice, The Intersection of Public Speaking, Action, and Authentic Leadership

Copyright © 2025 by Emmanuel Joseph

All rights reserved. No part of this publication may be reproduced, stored or transmitted in any form or by any means, electronic, mechanical, photocopying, recording, scanning, or otherwise without written permission from the publisher. It is illegal to copy this book, post it to a website, or distribute it by any other means without permission.

First edition

This book was professionally typeset on Reedsy.
Find out more at reedsy.com

Contents

1	Chapter 1: The Power of Authenticity in Leadership	1
2	Chapter 2: Finding Your Voice	3
3	Chapter 3: The Art of Storytelling	5
4	Chapter 4: Leading with Purpose	7
5	Chapter 5: The Impact of Non-Verbal Communication	9
6	Chapter 6: The Role of Emotional Intelligence	11
7	Chapter 7: Leading by Example	12
8	Chapter 8: The Power of Positive Reinforcement	13
9	Chapter 9: The Balance of Humility and Confidence	14
10	Chapter 10: The Role of Adaptability in Leadership	16
11	Chapter 11: The Importance of Vision in Leadership	18
12	Chapter 12: Building a Culture of Trust	20
13	Chapter 13: Empowering Others	22
14	Chapter 14: The Value of Transparency	24
15	Chapter 15: The Role of Innovation in Leadership	26
16	Chapter 16: The Impact of Resilience	28
17	Chapter 17: The Legacy of Leadership	29

1

Chapter 1: The Power of Authenticity in Leadership

In a world where leaders are often judged by their ability to inspire and influence, authenticity stands as a cornerstone of effective leadership. Authentic leaders are those who stay true to their values and principles, regardless of external pressures. They understand that their genuine self is their greatest asset, and they harness this authenticity to connect with their audience on a deeper level. This connection is not just about words; it's about the resonance of their voice, the sincerity of their actions, and the integrity of their leadership.

Authentic leadership begins with self-awareness. Leaders who know themselves— their strengths, weaknesses, and core values— are better equipped to lead with purpose and conviction. This self-awareness enables them to navigate the complexities of leadership with clarity and confidence. It allows them to make decisions that are aligned with their values, creating a sense of trust and credibility among their followers. When leaders are authentic, they inspire others to embrace their own authenticity, fostering a culture of openness and honesty.

Moreover, authentic leaders understand the importance of vulnerability. They are not afraid to show their true selves, even if it means revealing their imperfections. This vulnerability humanizes them and makes them more relatable to their audience. It breaks down barriers and builds bridges of trust and empathy. By being open about their struggles and challenges, authentic leaders create an environment where others feel safe to express their own vulnerabilities, leading to deeper connections and stronger relationships.

Finally, authenticity in leadership is about consistency. Authentic leaders walk their talk and align their actions with their words. This consistency reinforces their credibility and trustworthiness. People are more likely to follow leaders who consistently demonstrate their values and principles through their actions. Authenticity is not a one-time act; it's a continuous journey of staying true to oneself and leading with integrity. It is this steadfast commitment to authenticity that sets great leaders apart and makes their leadership truly impactful.

2

Chapter 2: Finding Your Voice

Public speaking is an art that can be mastered by anyone willing to invest the time and effort. However, the foundation of this art is the ability to find and use one's authentic voice. This voice is not just the physical sound produced by vocal cords but the unique expression of one's personality, beliefs, and values. It is through this authentic voice that leaders can genuinely connect with their audience and convey their message with clarity and conviction.

Finding your voice begins with introspection. It requires an honest assessment of who you are, what you stand for, and what you aim to achieve as a leader. This self-exploration helps in identifying your core message— the central theme that defines your leadership. When you speak from this core, your voice resonates with authenticity and passion. Your audience can sense this genuine commitment and is more likely to be inspired by your words.

Developing your voice also involves refining your communication skills. This includes honing your speaking techniques, such as tone, pitch, and pacing, as well as mastering non-verbal communication. Your body language, facial expressions, and eye contact all contribute to the impact of your message. By becoming aware of these elements and practicing them consistently, you can enhance your ability to convey your message effectively and authentically.

Moreover, finding your voice is about embracing your unique style. Every leader has a distinct way of expressing themselves, and it is this uniqueness that makes their voice powerful. Instead of imitating others, focus on developing your own style that reflects your personality and values. This authenticity will not only make you more relatable but also more memorable to your audience. It is through this unique voice that you can leave a lasting impression and make a meaningful impact.

3

Chapter 3: The Art of Storytelling

Storytelling is a powerful tool that leaders can use to engage, inspire, and influence their audience. A well-told story has the ability to evoke emotions, create connections, and drive action. It is through storytelling that leaders can bring their vision to life and make their message more relatable and impactful.

At the heart of storytelling is the ability to connect with your audience. This connection is built on empathy— the ability to understand and share the feelings of others. By putting yourself in the shoes of your audience, you can craft stories that resonate with their experiences and emotions. This empathy allows you to create a sense of shared understanding and build a stronger connection with your audience.

Effective storytelling also involves the use of vivid imagery and descriptive language. By painting a picture with your words, you can transport your audience into the world of your story. This vivid imagery helps in making your message more memorable and impactful. Additionally, the use of descriptive language allows you to convey complex ideas in a simple and engaging manner, making it easier for your audience to understand and relate to your message.

Moreover, storytelling is about authenticity. The most powerful stories are those that come from the heart and reflect genuine experiences and emotions. By sharing your own experiences and challenges, you can create a sense of authenticity that resonates with your audience. This authenticity not only makes your story more relatable but also builds trust and credibility. It is through these authentic stories that you can inspire and influence your audience effectively.

4

Chapter 4: Leading with Purpose

Purpose is the driving force behind effective leadership. It is the reason why leaders do what they do and the vision that guides their actions. Leading with purpose means having a clear understanding of your goals and a commitment to achieving them. It is this sense of purpose that gives leaders the motivation and determination to overcome challenges and inspire others to follow their lead.

At the core of purposeful leadership is the ability to articulate your vision. This vision is a clear and compelling picture of the future that you aim to create. By communicating this vision with passion and conviction, you can inspire others to join you in your journey. This shared vision creates a sense of purpose and direction, aligning the efforts of your team towards a common goal.

Leading with purpose also involves aligning your actions with your values. Authentic leaders stay true to their principles and make decisions that reflect their core values. This alignment creates a sense of integrity and consistency, building trust and credibility among your followers. When your actions are driven by purpose, you are more likely to make decisions that are in the best interest of your team and organization.

Moreover, purposeful leadership is about resilience. The journey towards achieving your vision is often filled with challenges and setbacks. It is during these times that your sense of purpose becomes your greatest asset. It gives you the strength and determination to persevere and continue moving forward. By staying true to your purpose, you can overcome obstacles and inspire others to do the same. It is this unwavering commitment to your purpose that sets great leaders apart and drives lasting success.

5

Chapter 5: The Impact of Non-Verbal Communication

While words are powerful, non-verbal communication plays an equally significant role in effective leadership. The way leaders carry themselves, their facial expressions, gestures, and body language, all contribute to the message they convey. Non-verbal communication can enhance or undermine the spoken word, making it a crucial aspect of leadership.

Non-verbal communication begins with self-awareness. Leaders who are aware of their body language can use it to reinforce their message and build a stronger connection with their audience. For example, maintaining eye contact conveys confidence and sincerity, while an open posture signals approachability and openness. By being mindful of these non-verbal cues, leaders can create a positive and engaging presence.

Moreover, non-verbal communication involves the ability to read and interpret the body language of others. Leaders who can understand the non-verbal signals of their team members are better equipped to address their concerns and needs. This ability to empathize and respond to non-verbal cues creates a sense of trust and understanding, fostering stronger relationships and collaboration.

Additionally, non-verbal communication is about consistency. Authentic leaders align their body language with their words, creating a coherent and believable message. Inconsistencies between verbal and non-verbal communication can create confusion and mistrust. By being consistent in their non-verbal cues, leaders can reinforce their message and build credibility.

6

Chapter 6: The Role of Emotional Intelligence

Emotional intelligence is the ability to recognize, understand, and manage one's own emotions and the emotions of others. It is a critical skill for effective leadership, as it enables leaders to navigate the complexities of human interactions and build strong relationships.

At the core of emotional intelligence is self-awareness. Leaders who are aware of their emotions can manage them effectively and prevent them from negatively impacting their decisions and actions. This self-awareness also allows leaders to understand their strengths and weaknesses, enabling them to lead with authenticity and confidence.

Empathy is another key component of emotional intelligence. Leaders who can empathize with others are better equipped to understand their needs, concerns, and motivations. This ability to connect with others on an emotional level fosters trust and loyalty, creating a positive and supportive work environment.

Furthermore, emotional intelligence involves effective communication. Leaders who can communicate with empathy and understanding are better able to inspire and motivate their team. By being attuned to the emotions of their audience, leaders can tailor their message to resonate with their feelings and create a more impactful connection.

7

Chapter 7: Leading by Example

Leading by example is one of the most powerful ways to inspire and influence others. Authentic leaders understand that their actions speak louder than their words, and they strive to model the behavior and values they want to see in their team.

Leading by example begins with integrity. Leaders who act with honesty and transparency build trust and credibility. By consistently demonstrating their values through their actions, leaders create a sense of trust and respect among their team members. This integrity serves as a foundation for strong and effective leadership.

Moreover, leading by example involves accountability. Authentic leaders take responsibility for their actions and decisions, and they hold themselves to the same standards they set for others. This accountability creates a culture of responsibility and excellence, encouraging team members to take ownership of their work and strive for continuous improvement.

Additionally, leading by example is about inspiring others. Leaders who demonstrate passion, dedication, and resilience in their work inspire their team to do the same. By showing what is possible through their actions, leaders motivate their team to reach their full potential and achieve their goals.

8

Chapter 8: The Power of Positive Reinforcement

Positive reinforcement is a powerful tool that leaders can use to motivate and inspire their team. By recognizing and rewarding positive behavior and achievements, leaders can create a supportive and encouraging work environment.

Positive reinforcement begins with recognition. Leaders who take the time to acknowledge and appreciate the efforts and contributions of their team members build a sense of value and belonging. This recognition can take many forms, from verbal praise to tangible rewards, and it serves to reinforce positive behavior and encourage continued excellence.

Moreover, positive reinforcement involves feedback. Authentic leaders provide constructive feedback that highlights strengths and areas for improvement. This feedback is delivered with empathy and understanding, creating a sense of support and encouragement. By providing regular and meaningful feedback, leaders can help their team members grow and develop their skills.

Furthermore, positive reinforcement is about creating a positive work culture. Leaders who foster a culture of appreciation and support create a more engaged and motivated team. This positive work environment not only enhances productivity but also promotes collaboration and innovation.

9

Chapter 9: The Balance of Humility and Confidence

Effective leadership requires a delicate balance of humility and confidence. Leaders who can navigate this balance inspire respect and admiration, creating a positive and empowering work environment. Humility and confidence are not mutually exclusive; they complement each other and enhance a leader's ability to connect with their team and drive success.

Humility in leadership begins with self-awareness. Leaders who are humble recognize their limitations and are open to feedback and learning. They acknowledge that they do not have all the answers and are willing to seek input and advice from others. This openness creates a sense of collaboration and fosters a culture of continuous improvement. Humble leaders are also more likely to build strong relationships based on trust and mutual respect.

Confidence, on the other hand, is about having faith in one's abilities and decisions. Confident leaders exude a sense of assurance and conviction that inspires others to follow their lead. This confidence is not about arrogance or bravado; it is about having a clear vision and the determination to achieve it. Confident leaders are decisive and take action, even in the face of uncertainty. This decisiveness builds trust and credibility, as others can rely on their leader to make informed and effective decisions.

CHAPTER 9: THE BALANCE OF HUMILITY AND CONFIDENCE

Moreover, the balance of humility and confidence involves authenticity. Authentic leaders stay true to their values and principles, regardless of external pressures. They lead with integrity and consistency, creating a sense of trust and credibility. By being humble and confident, leaders can create a positive and empowering work environment where team members feel valued and supported.

10

Chapter 10: The Role of Adaptability in Leadership

In a rapidly changing world, adaptability is a crucial trait for effective leadership. Leaders who can adapt to new situations and challenges are better equipped to navigate the complexities of their environment and drive success. Adaptability involves being open to change, embracing new ideas, and continuously learning and growing.

Adaptability begins with a growth mindset. Leaders with a growth mindset believe that their abilities and intelligence can be developed through effort and learning. They are open to feedback and view challenges as opportunities for growth. This mindset allows leaders to stay flexible and resilient in the face of change, enabling them to adapt to new situations and find innovative solutions.

Moreover, adaptability involves being proactive and forward-thinking. Effective leaders anticipate change and prepare for it, rather than reacting to it. They stay informed about trends and developments in their field and are willing to embrace new ideas and technologies. This proactive approach allows leaders to stay ahead of the curve and seize opportunities as they arise.

Additionally, adaptability is about being responsive to the needs of the team. Leaders who can adapt their leadership style to meet the needs of their team create a more supportive and inclusive work environment. This responsiveness fosters a sense of trust and collaboration, enabling the team to work together effectively and achieve their goals.

11

Chapter 11: The Importance of Vision in Leadership

A clear and compelling vision is a fundamental aspect of effective leadership. Vision provides a sense of direction and purpose, guiding the actions and decisions of leaders and their teams. It is through vision that leaders can inspire and motivate others to achieve their goals and create a meaningful impact.

Vision begins with clarity. Effective leaders have a clear understanding of their goals and objectives, and they can articulate this vision with passion and conviction. This clarity creates a sense of purpose and direction, aligning the efforts of the team towards a common goal. By communicating this vision effectively, leaders can inspire others to join them in their journey and work together towards achieving their objectives.

Moreover, vision involves foresight. Leaders with vision can anticipate future trends and developments, allowing them to make informed decisions and stay ahead of the curve. This foresight enables leaders to navigate the complexities of their environment and seize opportunities as they arise. By having a clear vision of the future, leaders can create a roadmap for success and guide their team towards achieving their goals.

Additionally, vision is about inspiration. A compelling vision has the power to evoke emotions and create a sense of excitement and motivation. Effective

CHAPTER 11: THE IMPORTANCE OF VISION IN LEADERSHIP

leaders can communicate their vision in a way that resonates with their audience, inspiring them to take action and work towards achieving their goals. This inspiration creates a sense of commitment and dedication, driving the team towards success.

12

Chapter 12: Building a Culture of Trust

Trust is the foundation of effective leadership and a critical component of a successful organization. Leaders who can build and maintain trust create a positive and empowering work environment where team members feel valued and supported. Trust is built through consistent actions, open communication, and a commitment to integrity and transparency.

Building trust begins with consistency. Leaders who consistently demonstrate their values and principles through their actions create a sense of reliability and credibility. This consistency reinforces the trust and respect of their team members, creating a strong foundation for effective leadership. By being consistent in their actions and decisions, leaders can build a culture of trust and accountability.

Moreover, trust involves open communication. Leaders who communicate openly and honestly with their team create a sense of transparency and openness. This communication fosters a culture of trust and collaboration, enabling team members to express their thoughts and ideas freely. By being open and transparent, leaders can build strong relationships based on trust and mutual respect.

Additionally, trust is about integrity. Authentic leaders stay true to their values and principles, regardless of external pressures. They act with honesty and transparency, creating a sense of trust and credibility. By demonstrating integrity in their actions and decisions, leaders can build a culture of trust and respect, fostering a positive and supportive work environment.

13

Chapter 13: Empowering Others

Empowerment is a key aspect of authentic leadership. Empowering others means giving them the tools, resources, and support they need to succeed. It involves fostering a sense of autonomy and encouraging team members to take ownership of their work. Leaders who empower others create a positive and collaborative work environment where everyone feels valued and motivated.

Empowering others begins with trust. Leaders who trust their team members create a sense of confidence and responsibility. This trust is built through consistent actions and open communication. By demonstrating trust in their team, leaders can empower them to take initiative and make decisions. This empowerment fosters a sense of ownership and accountability, leading to greater engagement and productivity.

Moreover, empowerment involves providing opportunities for growth and development. Authentic leaders invest in the growth of their team members by providing them with the resources and support they need to develop their skills. This investment in growth not only enhances the capabilities of the team but also creates a sense of loyalty and commitment. By empowering others to grow and succeed, leaders can create a positive and dynamic work environment.

Additionally, empowerment is about creating a culture of collaboration and support. Leaders who foster a collaborative environment encourage team members to work together and share their ideas and insights. This collaboration leads to greater innovation and creativity, driving the success of the organization. By empowering others to contribute and collaborate, leaders can create a positive and inclusive work culture.

14

Chapter 14: The Value of Transparency

Transparency is a fundamental aspect of authentic leadership. Leaders who are transparent in their actions and decisions create a sense of trust and credibility. Transparency involves open and honest communication, as well as a commitment to integrity and accountability. By being transparent, leaders can build strong relationships and foster a positive work environment.

Transparency begins with communication. Leaders who communicate openly and honestly with their team create a sense of trust and respect. This communication involves sharing information, explaining decisions, and being open to feedback. By being transparent in their communication, leaders can build a sense of trust and collaboration within their team.

Moreover, transparency involves accountability. Authentic leaders take responsibility for their actions and decisions, and they hold themselves to the same standards they set for others. This accountability creates a sense of trust and respect, as team members can rely on their leader to act with integrity and fairness. By being transparent and accountable, leaders can build a culture of trust and accountability within their organization.

Additionally, transparency is about integrity. Leaders who act with honesty and transparency create a sense of credibility and trustworthiness. This integrity is demonstrated through consistent actions and decisions that align with the leader's values and principles. By being transparent and acting with integrity, leaders can build strong relationships and foster a positive work environment.

15

Chapter 15: The Role of Innovation in Leadership

Innovation is a critical aspect of effective leadership. Leaders who embrace innovation are better equipped to navigate the complexities of their environment and drive success. Innovation involves being open to new ideas, embracing change, and fostering a culture of creativity and experimentation.

Innovation begins with a growth mindset. Leaders who believe in the potential for growth and development are more likely to embrace new ideas and take risks. This mindset allows leaders to stay flexible and adaptable, enabling them to navigate change and find innovative solutions. By fostering a growth mindset within their team, leaders can create a culture of continuous improvement and innovation.

Moreover, innovation involves being proactive and forward-thinking. Effective leaders anticipate change and prepare for it, rather than reacting to it. They stay informed about trends and developments in their field and are willing to embrace new ideas and technologies. This proactive approach allows leaders to stay ahead of the curve and seize opportunities as they arise.

Additionally, innovation is about fostering a culture of creativity and experimentation. Leaders who encourage their team members to think creatively and take risks create an environment where innovation can thrive.

CHAPTER 15: THE ROLE OF INNOVATION IN LEADERSHIP

This culture of creativity and experimentation leads to greater innovation and success. By embracing innovation, leaders can drive their organization towards continuous improvement and growth.

16

Chapter 16: The Impact of Resilience

Resilience is the ability to bounce back from setbacks and challenges. It is a critical trait for effective leadership, as it enables leaders to navigate the complexities of their environment and drive success. Resilience involves staying positive, maintaining perspective, and persevering in the face of adversity.

Resilience begins with a positive mindset. Leaders who stay positive and optimistic are better equipped to navigate challenges and setbacks. This positive mindset allows leaders to maintain perspective and focus on solutions rather than problems. By staying positive, leaders can inspire their team to persevere and continue moving forward.

Moreover, resilience involves maintaining perspective. Effective leaders understand that setbacks are a natural part of the journey towards success. They view challenges as opportunities for growth and learning, rather than obstacles. This perspective allows leaders to stay resilient and continue moving forward, even in the face of adversity.

Additionally, resilience is about perseverance. Leaders who persevere in the face of challenges demonstrate determination and commitment. This perseverance inspires others to stay resilient and continue working towards their goals. By demonstrating resilience, leaders can create a positive and supportive work environment where everyone feels motivated and empowered.

17

Chapter 17: The Legacy of Leadership

The legacy of leadership is the lasting impact that leaders leave behind. Authentic leaders understand that their actions and decisions have a long-term effect on their team and organization. They strive to create a positive and lasting legacy by leading with integrity, purpose, and authenticity.

The legacy of leadership begins with integrity. Leaders who act with honesty and transparency build trust and credibility. This integrity creates a positive and lasting impact on their team and organization. By leading with integrity, leaders can create a culture of trust and respect that endures long after they are gone.

Moreover, the legacy of leadership involves purpose. Authentic leaders have a clear understanding of their goals and objectives, and they lead with a sense of purpose and direction. This purpose drives their actions and decisions, creating a lasting impact on their team and organization. By leading with purpose, leaders can inspire others to continue working towards their vision and goals.

Additionally, the legacy of leadership is about authenticity. Leaders who stay true to their values and principles create a sense of trust and credibility. This authenticity creates a positive and lasting impact on their team and organization. By leading with authenticity, leaders can create a culture of openness and honesty that endures long after they are gone.

In conclusion, the legacy of leadership is the lasting impact that leaders leave behind. By leading with integrity, purpose, and authenticity, leaders can create a positive and lasting legacy that inspires and empowers others. It is through this legacy that leaders can make a meaningful and lasting impact on their team and organization.

Lead with Your Voice: The Intersection of Public Speaking, Action, and Authentic Leadership

In a world where leadership is often defined by charisma and influence, "Lead with Your Voice" delves into the essential elements that make a leader truly effective—authenticity, action, and the power of public speaking. This insightful book takes readers on a transformative journey, uncovering the secrets to becoming a leader who not only speaks with conviction but also leads with purpose and integrity.

Discover the power of your authentic voice and learn how to communicate with impact. Through introspection and self-awareness, you will uncover your unique style and master the art of storytelling, connecting with your audience on a deeper level. This book offers practical guidance on honing your communication skills, from refining your speaking techniques to harnessing the power of non-verbal communication.

Embrace the role of emotional intelligence and resilience in leadership, understanding how to navigate the complexities of human interactions and build strong relationships. Learn the importance of adaptability, vision, and innovation, and how these qualities drive success in a rapidly changing world. By balancing humility and confidence, you will inspire respect and admiration, creating a positive and empowering work environment.

"Lead with Your Voice" also emphasizes the significance of empowering others, fostering a culture of trust and collaboration. Through transparency, integrity, and positive reinforcement, you will create a lasting impact on your team and organization. This book provides valuable insights into building a legacy of leadership that endures long after your journey as a leader has begun.

Whether you are an aspiring leader or a seasoned professional, "Lead with Your Voice" offers a comprehensive guide to mastering the intersection of public speaking, action, and authentic leadership. Unleash the power of your voice and lead with authenticity and purpose.

www.ingramcontent.com/pod-product-compliance
Lightning Source LLC
LaVergne TN
LVHW020502080526
838202LV00057B/6105